COLL GRAMMAR RULES

Angus Rose and Richard Purkis

Series Editor
John McIlwain

Collins

Published by Collins Educational,
An imprint of HarperCollinsPublishersLtd
77–85 Fulham Palace Road,
London W6 8JB

www.collins.co.uk

© HarperCollinsPublishers Ltd

First published by © 1981 Shuter & Shooter (Pty) Ltd

This adaptation published in 1997 by © HarperCollinsPublishers Ltd

This edition published in 2005

10 9 8 7 6 5 4 3

ISBN-13 : 978-0-00-720537-0
ISBN-10 : 0-00-720537-6

British Library Cataloguing in Publication Data
A catalogue record for this book is available from the British Library.

Printed by Imago Ltd in Thailand

Contents

Section 1   The Word

A *Parts of speech*

English words can be divided into eight groups, known as the 'parts of speech':

- nouns
- pronouns
- verbs
- adjectives
- adverbs
- prepositions
- conjunctions
- interjections.

Each part of speech has its own job to do in a sentence.

Nouns name things.

'We thought we'd call him Noun.'

Nouns

Nouns are names. Nouns can be the names of people, places, things, groups, qualities, ideas.
There are four types of noun:

- proper
- common
- collective
- abstract.

Proper nouns

A proper noun names a person, group of people, place or thing:

Elvis Presley, the Beatles, Queen Victoria, London, Ramadan, Boeing 747, Africa

> **Remember** All proper nouns always begin with a capital letter:
> *Mickey Mouse* and *Roger Rabbit* went to *Disneyland Paris* and met *Goofy* at *Camp Davy Crockett*.

Common nouns

A proper noun tells you about one thing only, with its own name, but a common noun is just one of many things which all share the same features:

dog, flower, car, road, bacon

> **Remember** A common noun does not start with a capital letter (unless it begins a sentence).
> *A cannibal is a person who goes into a restaurant and orders the waiter.*

Collective nouns

A collective noun is the name of a group of people or things:

band (a group of musicians)
herd (a group of cows)
team (a group of sports players)
crew (a group of sailors)
audience, congregation, pack, gang

> **Remember** You can use collective nouns in either the singular or the plural – whichever you think sounds more suitable:
> Singular: *The band is playing at 9 o'clock.*
> Plural: *The band are going back to their homes for tea.*
> **But** don't mix singular and plural, like this:
> *The class left their seats before it was told to.*

Abstract nouns

An abstract noun is the name given to something that we can understand in our minds but cannot receive with our five senses. In other words we cannot see, hear, touch, taste or smell any abstract nouns:

excitement, courage, happiness, fear, misery, anger, hope, possibility

Abstract nouns do not start with a capital letter (unless they begin a sentence).

Just to confuse you

Some nouns, depending on how they are used, can fall into more than one group:

a pride of lions (collective)

full of pride (abstract)

Noun spotting: how to recognize a noun

There are several ways in which you can spot a noun in a sentence.

- Nouns usually have words like these immediately before them:

  a, an, the, some, any, my, his, her, their, this, that, those.

  a ball, the tractor, any news, my goodness, her house

- Some nouns have special endings:

  -tion: station, action, description

  -ness: happiness, emptiness, thickness

  -ism: magnetism, terrorism

  -or: doctor, actor, sailor

  -ing: swimming, eating, talking

You can find more tips in 'Spotting parts of speech – the question method' on page 27.

The features of nouns

Nouns have three chief features:
- countability (or non-countability)
- gender
- case.

Nouns are countable or uncountable.
A countable noun can be singular and plural:
car, cars
orange, oranges
An uncountable noun is singular only, with no plural:
happiness, beef, humour, sunlight

Just to confuse you

Some nouns look plural but have a singular meaning:

news, measles, physics, home economics

But some nouns are always plural and hardly ever have a singular meaning:

scissors, glasses (for eyesight), trousers, thanks

Nouns have a gender.
There are four main gender labels:
- masculine:
  man, boy, bull, sailor
- feminine:
  woman, girl, cow, actress
- neuter (neither masculine nor feminine):
  music, bucket, coffee, tent, gymnastics
- common (either masculine or feminine):
  child, person, athlete

Nouns have a case.
There are three main cases in English:
- subject (or nominative) case:
  The pencil broke.

- object (or accusative) case:
  Read the notice.
- possessive (or genitive) case:
  The team's kit, Sara's hat

To find out more about gender and cases, see page 48.

Plural nouns

The usual way to show a noun in the plural is to add an -*s*:
pen – pens; house – houses; train – trains
But there are many situations where this rule won't work:

- Nouns that end in -*ch, -s, -sh, -ss*, or -*x* add -*es* in the plural (If they didn't, we wouldn't be able to pronounce the plural.):
  pitch – pitches; bus – buses; gash – gashes; mattress – mattresses; fox – foxes
- Nouns ending in -*y*, with a consonant in front, change -*y* to -*ies* in the plural:
  baby – babies; pastry – pastries; party – parties
  However, nouns ending in -*y*, with a vowel in front, add -*s* in the plural as normal:
  donkey – donkeys; valley – valleys; Monday – Mondays
- Nouns ending in -*f* or -*fe* change to -*ves* in the plural:
  loaf – loaves; half – halves; wife – wives
  But even this rule won't always work:
  roof – roofs; chief – chiefs; safe – safes
- Most nouns that end in -*o* add -*es* in the plural:
  hero – heroes; tomato – tomatoes; potato – potatoes
- Some nouns are the same in the singular and the plural:
  one sheep, two sheep; one deer, two deer; one trout, two trout

---

Remember Never use an apostrophe (') to form plurals. Lots of adults do it, and they're wrong!

Pronouns

A pronoun is a word that is used instead of a noun. Pronouns produce sentences like this:

Mrs Jones told her son Ron to take his bike out of her car.

instead of awful ones like this:

Mrs Jones told Mrs Jones's son Ron to take Ron's bike out of Mrs Jones's car.

The types of pronoun

There are seven types of pronoun:
- personal
- possessive
- reflexive
- demonstrative
- interrogative
- relative
- indefinite.

Personal pronouns
Personal pronouns are used for people and things: I, me, you, he, she, it, we, us, you, they, them.

Possessive pronouns
Possessive pronouns show who or what owns them: mine, yours, hers, ours, theirs.

Remember Yours, hers, ours and theirs never have an apostrophe.

Reflexive pronouns
Reflexive pronouns link back to the subject: myself, yourself, himself, herself, itself, ourselves, yourselves, themselves.

I will do the job myself.
She saw herself on the TV.
You left yourselves with no chance.
They hid themselves.

Demonstrative pronouns
Demonstrative pronouns point out nouns or pronouns: this, that, these, those, them, such, one, ones, none.

This is the train for Dundee.
These are the keys.
Your bike is smaller than that.
Such is the case.

Interrogative pronouns
Interrogative pronouns ask questions:
who? which? what? whose?

Who paid?
Which have you bought?
What did you say?
Whose glasses are these?

Relative pronouns
Relative pronouns link people or things already mentioned:
who, which, whom, whose, that (sometimes).

The admiral, who by now had turned green, often gets seasick.
The car which I drive is an old banger.
The girl whom I mentioned is here.
The lady whose keys we needed was out.
The house that Jack built

Indefinite pronouns
Indefinite pronouns link people or things which are not exactly defined in number: anyone, someone, several, some, none, sometimes, one and they.

Can anyone hear me?
Someone belched. Who was it?
The noise upset several people. Some reacted angrily.
None of them was deafened.
One must not make rude noises.
They say the house is haunted.

The three persons of pronouns

Personal pronouns can be singular or plural. Each of these has three persons:

- 1st person singular (the person speaking or writing): *I*
- 2nd person singular (the person spoken to): *you*
- 3rd person singular (the person or thing spoken about): *he, she, it*
- 1st person plural: *we*
- 2nd person plural: *you*
- 3rd person plural: *they*.

Personal

	Person	Subject	Object	Possessive*	Reflexive
Singular	1	I	me	mine	myself
	2	you	you	yours	yourself
	3	he, she, it	him, her, it	his, hers, its	himself, herself, itself
Plural	1	we	us	ours	ourselves
	2	you	you	yours	yourselves
	3	they	them	theirs	themselves

* Look at Possessive Adjectives (page 15) as well.

Relative pronouns

Gende	Subject	Object	Possessive
Masc./Fem.	who	whom	whose
Neuter	which	which	whose

Demonstrative pronouns

	Singular	Plural
Nearby	this	these
Further away	that	those

Verbs

Verbs tell us about the action.

'Looks like I'm going to VERB you!'

Verbs are the most important words of all. Every sentence must have a verb in it.
Verbs can tell us two things:
- the *action* performed by a noun (or pronoun):
  The door <u>opened</u>. The milkman <u>entered</u>. I <u>thought</u> he was going to <u>cry</u>.
- the *state of being* of a noun (or pronoun):
  He <u>is</u> so upset. His van wheels <u>are</u> wobbly. He <u>will be</u> in trouble.

The main types of verb

There are three main types of verb:
- transitive
- intransitive
- auxiliary.

Transitive verbs
A transitive verb is followed by an object (see page 48). In other words, the action of a transitive verb does something to somebody or something.

Subject	*Verb*	*Object*
Rajiv	*helped*	*the old lady.*
The striker	*kicked*	*the ball.*

Intransitive verbs
An intransitive verb has no object. For example, you cannot shiver someone, or sneeze them.

Subject	Verb	No object
My granny	*shivered.*	–
The princess	*sneezed.*	–

Just to confuse you

Some verbs may be used transitively or intransitively, depending on the context:

Transitive	Intransitive
She <u>rang</u> the bell.	*The bell <u>rang</u>.*
I <u>opened</u> the door.	*The door <u>opened</u>.*

Auxiliary verbs
These are verbs which 'help' a participle or infinitive (see the panel on page 11 to make a complete verb. ('Auxiliary' means helping.)
The commonest auxiliary verbs are *be, have, must, may, can, do*:

It <u>is</u> raining.

I <u>have</u> opened my umbrella.

Bilal <u>ought</u> to open hers.

The rain <u>may</u> stop soon.

We <u>could</u> have sheltered.

It <u>does</u> look like stopping.

Two important parts of the verb

The infinitive

This is the base form of the verb, and usually has 'to' before it:

to fly, to waste, to swim, to ache.

The participle

There are two participles of any verb, the present participle and the past participle.

The present participle usually ends in -*ing*:

bathing, walking, writing, doing.

The past participle usually ends in -*ed*:

parted, dusted, rubbed, prepared.

The three main tenses

The tense of a verb shows when the action takes place (or will take place, or has taken place!). There are three main tenses:

- present
- past
- future.

Present tense

The present tense is used when the action is happening now:

I sing, I am singing, I do sing.

Past tense

The past tense is used when the action has already happened:

I sang, I was singing, I did sing, I had sung.

Future tense

The future tense is used when the action is going to happen:

I shall sing, I am going to sing, I am about to sing, I shall be singing.

Regular (or 'weak') verbs always behave like this:

Present tense	Past tense	Past participle	Future tense
I watch	I watched	[I have] watched	I shall watch
He plays	He played	[He has] played	He will play
They use	They used	[They have] used	They will use

Irregular (or 'strong' verbs) do not simply add -ed to the past forms. The verb itself changes.
(All good dictionaries show these changes.)

Present tense	Past tense	Past participle	Future tense
I sing	I sang	[I have] sung	I shall sing
He deals	He dealt	[He has] dealt	He will deal
We think	We thought	[We have] thought	We shall think
They eat	They ate	[They have] eaten	They will eat
Tom goes	Tom went	[Tom has] gone	Tom will go

King Concord!

The girls am going into town.

Dave are a good footballer.

Of course these are wrong! The concord rule is that a verb must always agree with its subject in person and number. If the subject is first singular, the verb must be in its first singular form; if it's second plural, the verb must be second plural ... and so on.

But when something is not certain, we break this rule:

If I were king ... (see page 55)

Other tenses: the perfect and the continuous

Besides the three main tenses, there are two other types you should know about:

• perfect

• continuous.

A tense is said to be *perfect* when the action is over and complete:

I have eaten; they were rewarded; you have been warned.

The past participle is always used for perfect tenses: *eaten, rewarded, warned*

A tense is said to be *continuous* when the action has been going on for some time, even though it may have started in the past:

Charlie is laughing. I have been waiting here for an hour (and am still waiting). Charlene had already been camping.

The present participle (-*ing*) is used to form continuous tenses.

Just to confuse you

Participles can be verbal nouns, as in:

Swimming is great exercise.

Many people enjoy dancing.

The dying and the dead lay on the battlefield.

(The posh name for verbal nouns is 'gerunds'.)

But always use a possessive adjective, not a pronoun, with a gerund:

I was sorry about his going (not 'him going').

Your saying that reminds me ... (not 'You saying').

Just to confuse you even more

Participles can be verbal adjectives, as in:

a swimming pool

a talking canary

a sunken wreck

a clapped-out old banger.

(The posh name for verbal adjectives is 'gerundives'.)

Voices

The 'voice' of a verb shows if the action is done by the subject, or whether the subject has the action done to it by someone or something else. There are two voices:
- active
- passive.

Active voice
Here the subject performs the action:
We read the play aloud. The sun shines. People breathe. They are speaking. You have helped him.

Passive voice
Here the subject has the action done to it by someone or something else (although the sentence may not always say who or what does the action):
The play was read aloud by the cast.
Diana was let down. (e.g. by her friend)
It has been decided, (e.g. by the committee)

Adjectives

Adjectives describe things.

Well...it's a very... ADJECTIVE painting.

Adjectives are words which tell us more about nouns or pronouns. An adjective is usually placed immediately in front of the word it describes:
a <u>lively</u> game show
<u>big</u> prizes
<u>Lucky</u> you!

The types of adjective

There are six main kinds of adjective:
- descriptive
- demonstrative
- possessive
- interrogative
- numerical
- quantitative.

Descriptive adjectives

Descriptive adjectives describe things. These are the most common type of adjective:

wonderful world, *happy* people, *wild* animals

Demonstrative adjectives

Demonstrative adjectives point out things:

this rain, *those* bends, *such* crazy driving

Look also at the panel on 'The articles' on page 16.

Possessive adjectives

Possessive adjectives show who or what owns them:

my fingers, *your* door, *their* parrot, *its* beak

Possessive 'its' **never** has an apostrophe:

The dog lost *its* bone.

Interrogative adjectives

Interrogative adjectives ask questions:

Which house? *Whose* car?

Numerical adjectives

Numerical adjectives show:
- number:
  seven birds, *one hundred* dancers, *each* pupil
- the order of things:
  first team, *second* thoughts, *final* whistle
- indefinite number:
  several problems, *some* ideas, *few* answers

Quantitative adjectives

Quantitative adjectives show how much of something:

a little bit of curry, more ice cream, a whole bar of chocolate, much pain

---

The articles

The articles *the, a* and *an* are all demonstrative adjectives.

The is known as the definite article.

A or *an* is the indefinite article.

We use *an* when the noun begins with a vowel:

An apple, an orange, an idiot.

Adjective spotting: how to recognize an adjective

Tip 1

Adjectives are usually placed immediately in front of the noun they refer to:

an enjoyable book

or they are linked to a noun by a verb:

Motorways are noisy.

Tip 2

You can often spot an adjective by its ending (suffix).

The most common are:

-able or -ible:	probable, terrible, likeable
-al:	general, actual, vital
-ary:	military, stationary
-en:	broken, fallen, sunken
-ful:	useful, awful, dreadful
-ic:	poetic, terrific, artistic
-ish:	childish, selfish, brownish
-ive:	active, persuasive, massive
-less:	hopeless, brainless, homeless
-ous:	serious, marvellous, famous
-some:	troublesome, handsome, loathsome
-y:	tricky, bumpy, rubbery

Comparison of adjectives

Adjectives have three degrees of comparison:
- positive
- comparative
- superlative.

Positive
This is the basic form of the adjective:
happy, old, honest

Comparative
This shows that the noun has more of the 'positive' quality:
happier, older, more honest

Superlative
This says that the noun has the maximum possible amount of the 'positive' quality:
happiest, oldest, most honest

The usual way to form the comparative and superlative is by adding -er and -est:
cold, colder, coldest

However, these rules won't always work:
- For adjectives which end in a consonant + *y*, drop the *y* and add *-ier* or *-est*:
  messy, messier, messiest; dry, drier, driest
- With long adjectives, or when to add *-er* and *-est* would sound awkward, then use *more* and *most*:
  honest, more honest, most honest
  horrible, more horrible, most horrible
  complimentary, more complimentary, most complimentary

- Some adjectives have irregular comparatives and superlatives:

Positive	Comparative	Superlative
good	better	best
many	more	most
little	less	least

Remember When you are comparing two things, use the comparative:

Dan is quite tall; but Harry is the taller.
Man. City were the better of the two teams.

When you are comparing three or more things, use the superlative:

This is the best answer of all.
This was the worst thing that could happen.

Adverbs

Adverbs tell us more about verbs.

Gloria glides **ADVERBIALLY** on the ice

Adverbs tell us more about verbs, and sometimes adjectives. Usually an adverb is as close to its verb as possible, and in front of other parts of speech:

He drove <u>dangerously</u>.
Sirius is a <u>very</u> bright star.
She spoke almost <u>inaudibly</u>.

The types of adverb   There are seven types of adverb:
- manner
- place
- time
- reason
- number
- degree
- negation.

Adverbs of manner
These answer the question 'How?':
Marge spoke <u>slowly</u>. The rescuers worked <u>furiously</u>.

Adverbs of place
These answer the question 'Where?':
Towser barked to go <u>outside</u>. Please stand <u>there</u>.

Adverbs of time
These answer the question 'When?':
I hope she arrives <u>soon</u>. Few girls are called Gertie <u>nowadays</u>.

Adverbs of reason
These answer the question 'Why?':
They were <u>therefore</u> promoted.
The meeting was cancelled <u>because of</u> the storm.

Adverbs of number
These answer the question 'How many?':
He did it <u>once</u>, but not <u>again</u>.

Adverbs of degree

These answer the questions 'How much?' or 'To what degree or extent?':

The bull was <u>very</u> annoyed.

Mrs Jones was <u>extremely</u> upset too.

Adverbs of negation

'Not' and sometimes 'neither … nor' are adverbs.

She would <u>not</u> laugh.

He <u>neither</u> sang <u>nor</u> whistled.

Adverbs can also …

… be added to adjectives, other adverbs, phrases and even whole sentences.

With other adverbs:

He spoke <u>painfully</u> slowly. The rider fell <u>quite</u> heavily.

With phrases:

The film about Humpty Dumpty was <u>completely</u> off the wall.

The driver was not <u>entirely</u> in the wrong.

With whole sentences:

Sensibly, Mrs Jones didn't annoy the bull any <u>further</u>.

Pigs <u>definitely</u> are not able to fly.

Adverb spotting: how to recognize an adverb

Tip 1

Most adverbs end in -*ly*. So to change an adjective into an adverb, we usually add -*ly*:

quick (adjective); *quickly* (adverb)

usual (adjective); *usually* (adverb).

Note the double 'l' in 'usually'.

> **Just to confuse you**
> * Because it ends in *-ly* doesn't mean it's an adverb! Look at these:
> *fly, lovely, bully, holy, ugly*
> * Some adverbs have their own special forms:
> *soon, now, here, also*
> * Some adverbs are the same as their adjectives:
> *fast, long, early, close, near*
> *A fast car* (adjective); *she drove fast* (adverb)
> *The early bird* (adjective); *they arrived early* (adverb).

Tip 2

Use the phrase 'in a ... way' instead of an adverb if you need to. This avoids trying to turn an adjective like 'lovely' into a gruesome (and non-existent) adverb like 'lovely'. It's much easier to say 'in a lovely way'.

Comparison of adverbs

Adverbs (like adjectives) have three degrees of comparison:
* positive
* comparative
* superlative.

Positive

This is the basic form of the adverb like those mentioned above:

soon, slowly, smoothly

Comparative

This gives the verb or adjective more of the 'positive' quality:

sooner; more slowly, more smoothly

Superlative

This says the verb or adjective has the maximum possible amount of the 'positive' quality:

soonest, most slowly, most smoothly

The usual ways of showing the comparative and superlative are:

- by adding -*er* and -*est* if the adverb has only one syllable:

  soon   sooner   soonest

  near   nearer   nearest

- by placing 'more' and 'most' in front of adverbs with more than one syllable:

  smoothly   more smoothly   most smoothly

  sincerely   more sincerely   most sincerely

Remember When you are comparing two situations use the comparative:

David eats <u>more greedily</u> than a hippopotamus.

Use the superlative to compare three or more situations, people, etc.:

Of all the staff, Mr Chatterjee teaches <u>most enthusiastically</u>.

Danger!

Never use an adjective where you need an adverb.

This is wrong:

He writes much neater.

It should be:

He writes much more neatly.

This is wrong too:

Why doesn't she speak proper?

It should be:

Why doesn't she speak properly?

Prepositions

Prepositions link one noun to another.

A preposition is a word which links two nouns (or pronouns):

The train went through the tunnel.

In this sentence *through* shows how 'train' and 'tunnel' are linked.

The girl was the daughter of a film star.

Here *of* links 'girl' with 'film star'.

Prepositions must go between the two nouns (or pronouns) they link, and immediately in front of the second one:

He dropped the banana from the window.

It fell in front of the bulldozer.

Prepositions include:
about, above, across, after, against, along, amid, around, at, before, behind, below, beneath, beside, between, beyond, by, down, except, for, from, in, inside, like, near, of, off, over, since, through, till, to, towards, under, until, up, upon, with.

Compound prepositions consist of more than one word:
apart from, because of, due to, in front of.

Just to confuse you

Many words can be used both as prepositions and adverbs:

He put a belt <u>round</u> his sagging trousers. (preposition)

She turned <u>round</u>. (adverb)

The best way to tell the difference is that a preposition must be followed by a noun, pronoun or similar phrase.

In the first example, 'round' is followed by 'his sagging trousers' so it must be a preposition.

Conjunctions

Conjunctions connect parts of a sentence.

Conjunctions are words which connect parts of a sentence. The main conjunctions are:
and, because, but, for, however, since, until, yet.

The types of conjunction

There are four types of conjunctions:
- co-ordinating
- contrasting
- co-relative
- subordinating.

Co-ordinating conjunctions

Co-ordinating conjunctions, such as *and, as* and

moreover, are used when the things joined are basically similar:

Both Butch <u>and</u> Tiddles like fish very much.
Butch likes fish, <u>as</u> does Tiddles.

Contrasting conjunctions

Contrasting conjunctions, such as *but, however* and *yet*, are used when the things joined are basically different:

I can't even ride a bike, <u>but</u> my granny is an astronaut.

Co-relative conjunctions

Co-relative conjunctions are used to emphasize that the two things joined are similar. Examples are *both + and; either + or; so + as; not only + but also*:

Grandpa wore <u>not only</u> a crash hat <u>but also</u> lycra shorts.

Subordinating conjunctions

Subordinating conjunctions, such as *after, because, for, since, till, when* and *although*, are used when one of the two things linked depends on the other:

<u>As</u> I walked out onto the stage, I was really nervous.
<u>Although</u> she could play hockey well, she preferred to watch.

In the first example, 'I was really nervous' is the main clause of the sentence. The clause 'As I walked out onto the stage' would not make sense without it.

For more on main and subordinate clauses, see page 54.

Danger!
Although conjunctions join things, they often start a sentence:

<u>While</u> in Paris, I went up the Eiffel Tower.
<u>As</u> Mummy was ill, I cooked lunch.

Interjections

Interjections are on their own and have no grammatical function.

Drat!

Interjections are usually words on their own, often used to express strong feelings:
Oh! Phew! Drat! Yippee! Hurrah! Hello.
They have no grammatical function and can occur almost anywhere in a sentence.
A: My grandad lived to be 104.
B: Really?
A: Yes, after 70 he never changed his socks.
B: Blimey!
A: His feet didn't half smell especially, yuk, at meal times.
B: Eargghhh!!!!

Spotting parts of speech – the question method

'Looks like the nouns have landed.'

If you need to know the different parts of speech in a sentence, try the suggestions below:

To spot a noun, ask 'What?', 'Who?' or 'Whom?' before the verb.

Nouns and pronouns To spot a noun or pronoun, ask the questions 'What?':
'Who?' or 'Whom?':
The elephant charged through the undergrowth.
What charged? ⟶ elephant (noun)
Through what? ⟶ undergrowth (noun)

She asked me about our holiday.
Who asked? ⟶ she (pronoun)
Whom did she ask? ⟶ me (pronoun)
What about? ⟶ holiday (noun)

Verbs To spot a verb, ask the question 'What does (or did) the subject do?':
She asked me if I was OK.
What did she do? ⟶ asked (verb)

But for a verb used in the passive voice (see page 14) we need to ask 'What was done to the subject?':
My ankle was broken by the tackle.
What was done to the ankle? ⟶ was broken (verb)

Tip
The intransitive 'being' verbs are difficult to spot unless you learn them. They are *to be* (*am, are, is, were*, etc.), *to appear, to seem.*
The house is green. She seems lonely. They appear normal.

Adjectives

To spot an adjective, ask the questions 'Which?', 'What kind of?' or 'How many?':
Those boys are working hard.
Which boys? ───────→ those (adjective)

The green apples stayed on the branches.
What kind of apples? ─→ green (adjective)

Three men entered the old house.
How many men? ──────→ three (adjective)
What kind of house? ─→ old (adjective)

Adverbs

• To spot an adverb, ask the questions 'How?', 'Where?', 'When?' or 'Why?':
Yesterday Mr Grotch's Rolls Royce rolled smoothly downhill, ending in the river.
How did it roll? ──────→ smoothly (adverb)
Where did it roll? ───→ downhill (adverb)
When did it roll? ────→ yesterday (adverb)

• But for adverbs of degree with verbs, ask the questions 'How much?' or 'To what extent?':
Mr Grotch was very annoyed.
How much was Mr Grotch annoyed? ──→very (adverb)

• For adverbs of degree with adjectives and adverbs, ask the question 'How?':
Her extremely old grandfather walked very slowly.
How old? ───────────→ extremely (adverb)
How slowly? ────────→ very (adverb)

Remember 'Not' is always an adverb.

Prepositions

To spot a preposition, look for more than one noun or pronoun in the sentence, then check to see if they are linked in some way. Then look for the word which shows how one is related to the other.

The box remained under the table.

The nouns are 'box' and 'table'; 'under' shows where the box is in relation to the table (and it is therefore a preposition).
Prepositions must (normally) be followed by a noun or pronoun.
('Pre' is Latin for 'in front of' so the name 'preposition' suggests a position in front of a noun or pronoun.)

B *Word building*
Affixes (Prefixes and Suffixes)

Roots are the basic parts of words.

'Not THAT sort of roof!'

A 'root' is a basic word from which other words are made. For example, the root word 'cover' can change to uncover, discover, recover, covering, rediscovery … and so on.
The new 'bits' of the word, *un-, dis-, -ing*, etc., are called 'affixes'. There are two sorts of affix:

• prefixes   • suffixes.

A prefix is a group of letters with a definite meaning, put in front of a root:
tele – vision, *anti* – septic, *geo* – graphy,
A suffix is a group of letters with a definite job to do, which is put after a root:
good – *ness*, million – *aire*, disturb – *ance*.

Building words with prefixes and suffixes

You can build words …
- with a prefix + root;
  semi + circle
- with a root + suffix
  laugh + able
- or even with a prefix + root + suffix
  under + stand + ing, re + cover + able.

Prefixes and their meaning

Try to learn as many prefix meanings as you can. This will help you guess the meaning of hundreds of words you didn't know before.
There are many prefixes. Here are just a few you'll come across:

Prefix	Meaning	Example
pre	before	pre-cook
anti	against	anti-aircraft
mis	wrong	misunderstand
multi	many	multicoloured
post	after	postscript
semi	half	semicircle

Prefix	Meaning	Example
con, con, co	with	contract
ex	out of	export
ad	to	admit

Dictionaries have prefixes as separate headwords. Use your dictionary whenever you meet a new prefix or a new root.

Suffixes and parts of speech

- The suffix -*ic* added to a noun makes an adjective:
  photograph (noun) + *ic* = *photographic* (adjective)
  scene (noun) + *ic* = *scenic* (adjective)
- The suffix -*or* makes a noun and means 'someone who does an action':
  sail (verb) + *or* = *sailor* (noun)
  direct (verb) + *or* = *director* (noun)
  conduct (verb) + *or* = *conductor* (noun)

Some common suffixes and what they do

- Make nouns:
  -er, -or buyer, tutor
  -ess actress, princess
  -ism magnetism, vandalism
  -ment ornament, pavement
  -ness goodness, wickedness
  -ice advice, practice
  -ship friendship, kinship
- Make verbs:
  -en frighten, strengthen
  -fy horrify, magnify

- Make adjectives:

    -able   lovable, drinkable

    -ful   beautiful, useful

    -less   helpless, harmless

- Make adverbs:

    -ly   quickly, strangely.

There are many more suffixes which you will meet.

Whenever you meet a new one, make a note of it and find out what part of speech it makes.

Just to confuse you

A derivative is a new word made when you can add a prefix to the root and sometimes a suffix too. Find out all the derivative words you can make from this table, e.g. photo + graph + y = photography.

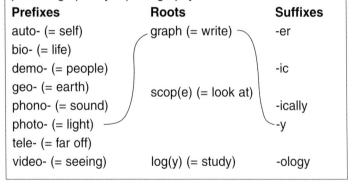

Prefixes	Roots	Suffixes
auto- (= self)	graph (= write)	-er
bio- (= life)		
demo- (= people)		-ic
geo- (= earth)	scop(e) (= look at)	
phono- (= sound)		-ically
photo- (= light)		-y
tele- (= far off)		
video- (= seeing)	log(y) (= study)	-ology

Compounds

Put words together to form compounds.

New words can also be made by joining two (or more) words together to form compounds. Compounds can be made with or without hyphens.

With hyphens:
long-ago, long-haired, long-winded, long-legged
See also page 63.

Without hyphens:
starfish, starship, stardust, starboard

> **Just to confuse you**
> Compound words often have a totally different meaning from the original words used to form them:
> *hopscotch, sou'-wester, horseplay*

C Spelling guide
Three hints for better spelling

1. Poor speech makes for poor spelling. Speak clearly, even inside your own head, and this will help your spelling.
   Dictionaries often tell you how to say words properly (see page 40).

Just to prove it
These three words are often wrongly spelled because they are wrongly pronounced:
specific, undoubtedly, pronunciation

2. Most strangely spelled words in English have come from other languages:
   Suede (pronounced *swayed*), the non-shiny leather, comes from the French 'suéde' meaning Sweden, where this sort of clothing first came from.
   Disciple, a follower, comes from the Latin 'discipulus', meaning a person who learns.
   Good dictionaries often show the origins of words.

3. Train yourself to 'photograph' words which present spelling problems. Do this by forming a clear picture of them in your mind. Don't be afraid to make up your own aids to memory. For instance:
   Parallel has two parallel lines in the middle of it.

Don't be afraid to make up your own spelling aids to memory.

Eleven general rules

Don't forget that, with English words, there are always some exceptions to every rule. You need to learn the exceptions as well as the rules.

1. When a word with one syllable ends in a vowel + a consonant (e.g. *hop*), *double the consonant* when you add a suffix: *hopping*

shop	*shopping*
strap	*strapped*
bat	*batted*
bag	*baggy*
sad	*sadden*

Think what these words would sound like if you **didn't** double the consonant.

But if the suffix itself begins with a consonant this rule does not apply:

sad	*sadly*

2. When a word has more than one syllable and the accent falls on the last syllable, *double the final consonant.*

refer	*referring*
fulfil	*fulfilled*
occur	*occurring*

3. In words of more than one syllable, a short vowel is frequently followed by a *double* consonant:

Short vowel		**Long vowel**
hopping	but	*hoping*
cattle	but	*cater*
carry	but	*caring*
dinner	but	*dining*

4. In words ending with one 'l', double the 'l' when a suffix is added:

travel	*traveller*
marvel	*marvellous*

But this rule doesn't apply to American spellings.

5. The final 'y' after a consonant becomes 'i' when a suffix is added:

beauty	*beautiful*
bury	*buried*
lovely	*lovelier*

See also plurals, page 5.

But the suffix '-ing' keeps the 'y' because of pronunciation:

carry   carried but *carrying*
steady steadier but *steadying*

6. The 'e' after a consonant is usually dropped when the suffix starts with a vowel, but kept when the suffix starts with a consonant:
   use   using but *useful*
   care   caring but *careful*

Remember There are many exceptions to this rule:
likeable
sizeable
ageing
singeing

---

7. The 'e' after consonants 'c' and 'g' is usually kept; it is also kept with the suffixes *-able, -ous*:
   change   changeable
   notice   noticeable
   courage   courageous

8. When a compound word is formed by adding a prefix or suffix ending in 'll', only one 'l' is kept:
   well + *come* = *welcome*
   all   + *ways* = *always*
   care + *full* = *careful*
   peace + *full* = *peaceful*
   skill + *full* = *skilful*
   But there are exceptions:
   full + *ness* = *fullness*
   still + *ness* = *stillness*

9. 'i' before 'e' except after 'c' when the sound is 'ee':
Not after 'c': *brief, mischief, piece, field, niece*
After 'c': *receive, deceive, conceited, ceiling*
But not where the sound is not 'ee':
science, foreign, leisure, height

Remember 'seize' and 'weird' are exceptions to the rule.

---

10. Verbs ending in 'c' add 'k' before suffixes beginning with a vowel:

picnic	*picnicker*
panic	*panicking*
frolic	*frolicked*

11. Verbs ending in 'ie' change to 'y' when adding suffix is '-ing':

lie	*lying*
die	*dying*
tie	*tying*

Remember When adding prefixes and suffixes, be sure to carry over all of the affix:

accidental	+	*ly*	=	*accidentally*
real	+	*ly*	=	*really*
cool	+	*ly*	=	*coolly*
over	+	*run*	=	*overrun*
il	+	*literate*	=	*illiterate*
un	+	*noticed*	=	*unnoticed*
mean	+	*ness*	=	*meanness*
book	+	*keeping*	=	*bookkeeping*
dis	+	*satisfied*	=	*dissatisfied*

When you learn a new spelling, always practise it in a sentence; then you will learn its meaning as well.

D *Using a dictionary*

Dictionaries can be very useful.

Dictionaries contain far more than just the spellings and meanings of words.

The words are listed in alphabetical order. In a good dictionary you will find:

- headword
- plural
- part of speech
- definition
- origin
- compounds and derivatives
- comparative and superlative form of adjectives and adverbs
- phrases and idioms.

Adult dictionaries also supply pronunciations.

north-westerly 480 noticeboard

north-westerly
1 (adjective) North-westerly means to or towards the north-west.
2 A north-westerly wind blows from the north-west.

north-western
(adjective) in or from the north-west.

Norwegian, Norwegians (pronounced nor-**wee**-jn)
1 (adjective) belonging or relating to Norway.
2 (noun) A Norwegian is someone who comes from Norway.
3 Norwegian is the main language spoken in Norway.

nose, noses, nosing, nosed
1 (noun) Your nose is the part of your face above your mouth which you use for smelling and breathing.
2 The nose of a car or plane is the front part of it.
3 (phrase) If you **pay through the nose** for something, you pay a very high price for it.
4 If someone **turns their nose up at** something, they reject it because they think it is not good enough for them.
5 (verb; an informal use) If someone noses into something, they try and find out about it when it is none of their business.

nosedive, nosedives
(noun) A nosedive is a sudden downward plunge by an aircraft.

nostalgia (pronounced nos-**tal**-ja)
(noun) Nostalgia is a feeling of affection for the past, and sadness that things have changed.
nostalgic (adjective), **nostalgically** (adverb).

nostril, nostrils
(noun) Your nostrils are the two openings in your nose which you breathe through.
[from Old English *nosu* meaning 'nose' and *thyrel* meaning 'hole']

nosy, nosier, nosiest; also spelled **nossy**
(adjective) trying to find out about things that do not concern you.

not
(adverb) used to make a sentence negative, to refuse something, or to deny something.

notable
(adjective) important or interesting, e.g. *With a few notable exceptions this trend has continued.*
notably (adverb).

[from a mistaken division of Middle English *an otch*]

note, notes, noting, noted
1 (noun) A note is a short letter.
2 A note is also a written piece of information that helps you to remember something, e.g. *I'll make a note of that.*
3 A note is also a banknote.
4 In music, a note is a musical sound of a particular pitch, or a written symbol that represents it.
5 A note is also an atmosphere, feeling, or quality, e.g. *There was a note of triumph in her voice . . . This was a good note on which to end.*
6 (verb) If you note a fact, you become aware of it or you mention it, e.g. *His audience, I noted, were looking bored.*
7 If you note something down, you write it down so that you will remember it.
8 (phrase) If you **take note** of something, you pay attention to it, e.g. *I had started taking note of political developments.*
[from Latin *nota* meaning 'mark' or 'sign']

note down
(phrasal verb) If you note something down, you write it down so that you will remember it.

notebook, notebooks
(noun) A notebook is a small book for writing notes in.

noted
(adjective) well-known and admired, e.g. *a noted American writer.*

noteworthy
(adjective) interesting or significant, e.g. *a noteworthy fact.*

nothing
(pronoun) not anything, e.g. *There's nothing to worry about.*

Similar words: zero, nought, nil, naught

notice, notices, noticing, noticed
1 (verb) If you notice something, you become aware of it.
2 (noun) Notice is attention or awareness, e.g. *Many cases have come to my notice.*
3 A notice is a written announcement.
4 Notice is also advance warning about something, e.g. *She could have done it if she'd had a bit more notice.*

Alphabetical order

A dictionary, like most reference books, is in alphabetical order. You would look up the word 'nosy' like this:

1. Find all the 'n' words.
2. Going by the second letter, find the 'no' words,
   e.g. no, nobility, noble …
3. Going by the third letter, find the 'nos' words,
   e.g. nose, nosedive, nostalgia …
4. Going by the fourth letter, find 'nosy'!

Tip 1

To look up words fast, use the guide words at the top of each dictionary page. They tell you the first and last words on the page. If the word you want doesn't come alphabetically between those two words, then it isn't on that page.

Pronunciation

As well as giving the meaning of words, dictionaries usually show how they should be said or *pronounced.* There are two common ways of showing how words are pronounced:

• phonetic (using Roman alphabet)
• the International Phonetic Alphabet.

When the pronunciation is shown phonetically, the word is re-spelled as we say it. It is divided into syllables with a stress mark (′) after a syllable– which must be emphasized:

Norwegian (Nawwē′jun);
alphabet (al′-fuh-bet)

The International Phonetic Alphabet is a more accurate system of letters and symbols which makes it possible to pronounce any word in most of the world's languages (not just English).

The mark (′) goes before the syllable to be stressed:

Norwegian (nɔː′wiːdʒən);
alphabet (′ælfəˌbɛt)

Tip 2

For just one week, take 10 minutes a day to practise opening your dictionary at the right letter. Give yourself 10 points for a direct hit, with marks knocked off for a near miss, bad miss, hopeless guess, etc.

Tip 3

To save space, not every word is listed separately in a dictionary. For example, 'leakage' is found under 'leak'; 'sickness' is found under 'sick'. 'Leak' and 'sick' are the *headwords*.

Parts of speech

Any good dictionary will list meanings of words under parts of speech. Take a look at this entry:

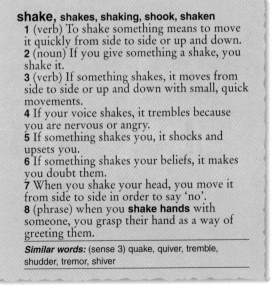

shake, shakes, shaking, shook, shaken
1 (verb) To shake something means to move it quickly from side to side or up and down.
2 (noun) If you give something a shake, you shake it.
3 (verb) If something shakes, it moves from side to side or up and down with small, quick movements.
4 If your voice shakes, it trembles because you are nervous or angry.
5 If something shakes you, it shocks and upsets you.
6 If something shakes your beliefs, it makes you doubt them.
7 When you shake your head, you move it from side to side in order to say 'no'.
8 (phrase) when you **shake hands** with someone, you grasp their hand as a way of greeting them.

Similar words: (sense 3) quake, quiver, tremble, shudder, tremor, shiver

Can you spot meanings of 'shake' (a) as a noun, (b) as a transitive verb, (c) as an intransitive verb?

fast, faster, fastest; fasts, fasting, fasted
1 (adjective and adverb) moving, doing something, or happening quickly or with great speed.
2 If a clock is fast, it shows a time that is later than the real time.
3 A fast film is very sensitive and can be used for taking photographs in low-light conditions.
4 A fast way of life involves a lot of enjoyable and expensive activities, e.g. *She wanted to move in the fast set.*
5 (adverb) Something that is held fast is firmly fixed.
6 (phrase) if you are **fast asleep**, you are in a deep sleep.
7 (adjective) Fast colours or dyes will not run or come out when wet.
8 (verb) If you fast, you eat no food at all for a period of time, usually for religious reasons.
9 (noun) A fast is a period of time during which someone does not eat food.

Similar words: (sense 1) quick, fleet, speedy, quickly, rapidly, swiftly

Can you spot meanings of 'fast' (a) as an adjective (also its comparative and superlative forms), (b) as an adverb, (c) as an intransitive verb (and its present and past participles)?

Phrases and idioms

'That'll be fifty pounds'

Every language has expressions which cannot be translated word for word into another language. These are called idioms.

Look back to page 39 where the headword 'nose' is printed. Find the following idioms:
(a) to pay through the nose
(b) to turn up one's nose.

In your own dictionary, look up the special (idiomatic) meanings of the following:
(a) to be all ears
(b) feel your ears burning
(c) have an ear to the ground
(d) wet behind the ears.

Note how they are used in sentences.
There is more about idioms on page 81.

Word origins

You can have a lot of fun finding out where words come from and how they got their present meaning in English. For each entry, most good dictionaries give a word's original language(s) and its meaning in that language.

Look where the word 'shillyshally's came from:

> **shillyshally, shillyshallies, shillyshallying, shillyshallied**
> (verb) If you shillyshally, you hesitate a lot and cannot make a decision.
> [from an 18th century expression '*to go, shill I, shall I*' meaning 'shall I or shan't I go']

Other dictionary pages

In most good school dictionaries there is a lot of valuable information (abbreviations, word lists, etc.) at the front and back of the book too.

Many dictionaries include, in a separate section:
• a list of common abbreviations
• a list of words and meanings too new to be in the main dictionary
• a list of foreign words and phrases used, as they stand, in English
• a short history of the English language
• weights and measures
and many other types of interesting information.

E *Synonyms and antonyms*

Synonyms are words that mean the same as one another.

That's hilarious!

That's FUNNY!

A *synonym* is a word meaning the same as another word.

An *antonym* is a word meaning the opposite of another word.

Using a thesaurus to find synonyms

Dictionaries give synonyms and sometimes antonyms along with a lot of other information. A thesaurus is an equally useful book which simply lists words of similar and opposite meanings.

Modern thesauruses list headwords alphabetically in the main part of the book.

The first thesaurus, written by Peter Mark Roget, lists synonyms in numbered sections. You look up your word in the index at the back. This refers you by number to the section you want in the main part of the book.

visit v. **1.** be the guest of, call in, call on, drop in on (*Inf.*), go to see, inspect, look (someone) up, pay a call on, pop in (*inf.*), stay at, stay with, stop by, take in (*Inf.*) **2.** afflict, assail, attack, befall, descend upon, haunt, smite, trouble **3.** *With* **on** *or* **upon** bring down upon, execute, impose, inflict, wreak ~ *n.* **4.** call, sojourn, stay, stop
visitation 1. examination, inspection, visit **2.** bane, blight, calamity, cataclysm, catastrophe, disaster, Infliction, ordeal, punishment, scourge, trial
visitor caller, company, guest, visitant

Making antonyms

Opposites (antonyms) are most often formed by adding prefixes to root words (see page 29):

im	+	*possible*	=	*impossible*
non	+	*sense*	=	*nonsense*
un	+	*usual*	=	*unusual*
il	+	*legal*	=	*illegal*
dis	+	*honest*	=	*dishonest*
in	+	*complete*	=	*incomplete*

The suffix -less is also used to form antonyms:

worth +	*less*	=	*worthless*
harm +	*less*	=	*harmless*
brain +	*less*	=	*brainless*

Just to confuse you

Affixes like *in-* and *-less* do not always make a word opposite to the root word. For example, 'invaluable' and 'priceless' both mean so valuable that they cannot be given a high enough price. 'Countless' and 'innumerable' both mean 'too many to be counted'.

Remember always to check the meanings of new words before you use them.

Section 2

Word Groups and the Sentence

A *The sentence*

Word order

The order of words can make a big difference.

Dog bites postman   Postman bites dog

In some languages, the order of words in a sentence is unimportant, and does not change its meaning.

In English, the order and position of words matter. Change either of these and you change what the sentence means.

For example, look how the meaning changes as we swap these words around:

The man walked his pet dog.
The pet dog walked his man.
The dog walked his pet man.
Walked pet the man dog his.

Normal word order   The normal word order is Subject – Verb – Object.

Subject

The subject is a noun, pronoun or noun phrase (see page 51) about which we are making a statement:

My <u>mountain bike</u> has 16 gears.
The <u>video camera</u> helped to catch the shoplifter.

Verb

Information on the verb can be found in Section A: Parts of Speech (pages 9–14).

Object

The object is the noun or pronoun to which the action of the verb is being done:

The donkey ate the <u>carrot</u>.
Donna picked a <u>bunch of daisies</u>.
My dog loves <u>me</u>.

There are two types of object:
• direct
• indirect.

A direct object is a person or thing directly affected by the action of the verb:

Birds eat <u>worms</u>.

An indirect object is a person or thing for whom the action of the verb and its object is done:

He gave <u>Lennie</u> a map.
He gave a map to <u>Lennie</u>.

The indirect object normally comes between the verb and the direct object (unless you use 'for' or 'to').

Extras: predicate and complement
Predicate

The predicate is the rest of the sentence after the subject:

Tess thinks that Indian food is great.

In this sentence 'thinks that Indian food is great' is the predicate. It includes the verb and the object.

Complement

The complement is the words after the verb or object which are needed to complete the predicate (to make the sentence make full sense):

I like nasty people to be punished.

In this sentence 'to be punished' is the complement. Left on its own, 'I like nasty people' wouldn't give the meaning you want!

Remember

- Every sentence needs a verb.
- Every sentence has a predicate (even if it is only one or two words).
- Sentences do not need to have an object or a complement.

Changing word order

If we change the normal word order of Subject – Verb – Object we change the meaning.

The commonest change is to Verb – Subject – Object to form a question.

Statement:

Subject	Verb	Object
You	*have never eaten*	*frog's legs.*

Question:

Verb	Subject	Object
Have	*you never eaten*	*frog's legs?*

You can also change word order for effect. A sentence such as:

'No!' was his definite answer.

can be made stronger like this:

His answer was a definite 'No!'

Word order and parts of speech

The position of a word in a sentence normally decides what job it does. Look at what happens to the word 'round' in these sentences. Think what part of speech it is in each case (answers below the sentences).

1. *The round of applause lasted for five minutes.*
2. *Yachts round the buoy before the finish.*
3. *The round table stood in Camelot.*
4. *We walked round to my Gran's.*
5. *You must run round the track.*

1. noun (in subject position)
2. verb (in verb position)
3. adjective (next to noun 'table')
4. adverb (next to verb 'walked')
5. preposition (relates subject 'you' to 'track')

Word order and modifiers

Any word which modifies (see box below) another word in a sentence must be placed as closely as possible to the word it modifies. In these sentences 'only' modifies different words, giving us different meanings:

My only sister likes jazz. (I have no other sister.)
My sister only likes jazz. (Nobody in the family except my sister likes jazz; or she just likes jazz, but isn't crazy about it.)
My sister likes only jazz. (She doesn't like other music.)
My sister likes jazz only. (Same as the last example, but the statement is more emphatic.)

Modifiers

To 'modify' a word means to add extra meaning to it.

In the phrase 'a red car', the word 'red' modifies 'car' by telling us more about it.

In the sentence 'We quickly scored 50 runs', the word 'quickly' modifies 'scored'.

A modifier is any word which adds extra meaning to another.

Phrases

A phrase is any group of words which, taken together in a sentence, functions as a part of speech.

Noun phrases

A noun phrase is a group of words acting together as a noun:

Riding a bicycle requires skill.

Here the phrase 'Riding a bicycle' forms the subject and acts as a noun.

Remember that the question 'What?' is one way to test for nouns: see page 27.

A noun together with its adjectives (whether single or a phrase) is also referred to as a noun phrase:

That barking dog from next door keeps me awake at night.

Adjective phrases

A group of words acting together as an adjective is known as an adjective phrase:

The man with the tall white hat is the chef.

Here the phrase 'with the tall white hat' tell us which man and therefore functions as an adjective.

Remember that the question 'Which?' is one way to test for adjectives: see page 28.

Verb phrases

A verb phrase is a group of words forming a verb:

I shall be going to town tomorrow.

Here the auxiliary verb 'shall be' and the present participle 'going' are both necessary to show that the action is in the future.

Remember that the question 'What does (or did) the subject do?' is one way to test for verbs: see page 27.

> **Phrasal verbs**
> Often a verb is added to an adverb to give a special meaning, such as 'up' in this sentence:
> *Please shut up!*
> Here the phrasal verb 'shut up' means 'be quiet' – very different from the normal meaning of 'to shut'.
> There are hundreds of phrasal verbs, including: turn out, write off, step up, square up, polish off, run down. Try to think of some more examples.

Adverb phrases

An adverb phrase is a group of words acting as an adverb:

Gran was snoring <u>in bed</u> last night.

The phrase 'in bed' describes where the verb is happening.

Remember that the question 'Where?' is one way to test for adverbs: see page 28.

Clauses

When a phrase contains a verb it is called a clause.

Clauses form part of sentences.

There are three main types of clause:
- noun clauses
- adjectival clauses
- adverbial clauses.

Noun clauses

In the following sentence the underlined group of words contains the verb 'knew' and forms the subject of the verb 'was':

<u>What my brother knew about pop music</u> was next to nothing.

In the next sentence the underlined group of words contains the verb 'are going' and forms the object of the verb 'to know':

I want to know <u>where you are going</u>.

Adjectival clauses

The underlined clause in the next example tells us which man we are concerned with, and does the work of an adjective. It is a clause because it contains the verb 'is wearing'.

The man <u>who is wearing the purple bobble hat</u> is my dad.

There are two types of adjectival clauses:
- defining
- non-defining.

Defining clauses are necessary to our understanding of the noun described:

The man <u>who is wearing the purple bobble hat</u> is my dad.

Non-defining clauses merely give extra information that is not necessary to the meaning of the sentence:

Most dads, <u>who don't usually wear purple bobble hats</u>, aren't as crazy as mine.

> **Remember** Non-defining clauses must be enclosed in commas or brackets.

Adverbial clauses

There are eight types of adverbial clauses, those of:
- Time: These answer the question 'When?':
  He sent a fax <u>as soon as he arrived</u>.
- Place: These answer the question 'Where?':
  The boy stood <u>where the burning deck was coolest</u>.
- Reason: These answer the question 'Why?':
  The jockey was wearing pyjamas <u>because the horse always came in so late</u>.
- Purpose: These answer the question 'For what purpose?':
  He killed his parents <u>so he could go on the orphans' picnic</u>.
- Result: These answer the question 'With what results?':
  My house was so scruffy <u>that some vandals broke in and decorated it</u>.

- Condition: These answer the question 'Under what conditions or circumstances?':
  If you steal that calendar, you'll get 12 months!
- Concession: These usually begin with 'though' or 'although' (or similar conjunctions) and indicate 'granting certain circumstances':
  Though I tried to play the piano, I failed miserably.
- Comparison: In these clauses two things or ideas are compared or contrasted:
  The food is not as good as it used to be.

Main and subordinate clauses

In a sentence with two clauses, one is often the main clause and the other is the subordinate clause:

Subordinate	**Main**
As I was going to Paddock Wood,	
I met a girl named Suzie Hood.	

The second clause is the main one because it could stand on its own as a sentence. The first one could not stand on its own.

But sometimes the main clause is split, with the subordinate clause in the middle:

Main (1st part)   Subordinate   Main (2nd part)

That man over there,

wearing the purple bobble hat,

is my dad.

Types of sentence

There are
different types
of sentence.

That's cool!   Yes, but what IS it?

There are five types of sentence:
- statements   • exclamations
- questions   • wishes.
- commands

Statements
In statements the order of words is Subject – Verb – Object:
Cows eat grass.

Questions
In questions the order is Verb – Subject – Object:
Do elephants eat spaghetti?

Commands
Commands are also known as 'imperatives':
Don't swallow that spanner!

Exclamations
Exclamations are phrases used as interjections:
What an idiot I've been!

Wishes
In these sentences the concord rule (see page 12) sometimes seems to be broken. This is because the verb is being used in a special way, called the 'subjunctive mood':
If only I were old enough, I would join the air force.
May you have long life and happiness.

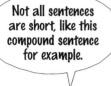

Not all sentences are short, like this compound sentence for example.

The construction of sentences

Simple sentences

These make sense by themselves and contain only one verb. Not all of them are short!

Most dogs are friendly.

Did you hear the one about the Englishman, the Irishman and the Scotsman?

Boiling with rage at the defendant's impertinence and controlling himself with difficulty, the judge ordered the court to be cleared.

Compound sentences

These are formed when two or more simple sentences are joined by a conjunction (such as 'and', 'but', 'because' etc.) or by suitable punctuation (see page 60):

Jack fell down and broke his crown.

Jack fell down, broke his crown and was carried off yelling.

Notice that here we do not have to repeat 'Jack' three times, because each clause has Jack as its subject.

Complex sentences

Sentences can be made up of a single clause plus one or more noun, adjectival or adverbial clauses:

Main clause	Subordinate clause
You ought to be on TV,	*so we could turn you off!*

'You ought to be on TV' is the main clause; the rest is a subordinate clause (see the box on page 54).

Sentences and style *Tip 1*

Improve your writing style by using more complex sentences.

- **Poor**: *I was eager to get up this morning. A carpet of dazzling white snow lay thickly outside my window.*
- **Better**: *Because a carpet of dazzling white snow lay outside my window, I was eager to get up this morning.*

The two simple sentences in the first version don't show that one was the cause of the other. The complex sentence of the second version does.

Tip 2

To add punch to your writing, put the main clause at the end:

- **For emphasis**: *Until you stop smoking, don't complain about your cough!*
- **For suspense**: *In the very doorway on the street where Sikes was to have handed over the stolen goods, there stood a policeman.*

Loose, periodic and balanced sentences

A *loose* sentence is one where the main clause comes first (i.e. before any subordinate clauses):

Look both ways, if you want to stay safe.

A *periodic* sentence is one where the main clause or the verb comes at the end. (Americans use the word 'period' instead of 'full stop'):

If you want to stay safe, look both ways.

A *balanced* sentence occurs when two or more clauses have equal importance:

Emperor Nero fiddled while Rome burned.

B *Punctuation*

Punctuation is very important. We put punctuation marks in our writing to make it easier to read and understand. Correct punctuation can make all the difference to meaning. These two examples have the same words but totally different meaning:

What do you think? I will feed you for nothing!
(A good offer.)
What! Do you think I will feed you for nothing!
(Not such a good offer!)

Ending a sentence

Sentences end with a punctuation mark.

Jack and Emma   . . . are friends!

Almost all sentences are closed by one of the following:

- Full stop (.):
  This sentence ends with a full stop and here it comes now.
- Question mark (?):
  What goes 'Ha-ha plonk'?
- Exclamation mark (!):
  What a fantastic joke!

Remember Only direct questions end with a question mark. This sentence is not direct and so doesn't need one:
I asked what went 'Ha-ha plonk'.

Just to confuse you
If a questioning sentence is more of an exclamation than a question, then end it with an exclamation mark:
Who do you think you are! What about that!

Some other sentence endings are found less often:

- Direct speech (' or "): When a sentence ends with direct speech (the actual words somebody speaks) then the quotation marks often end the sentence by coming after the punctuation mark:
  She said nervously, 'I'm just a harmless pupil. Why are you confusing me with all this grammar?'
  For more about the punctuation of direct speech, see page 66.
- Dash (–) A dash is used when someone is interrupted in mid-sentence either by another speaker or by a sudden thought, event, etc.:
  'The cabin's on fire and the ship's going to –'
  Abruptly, the commander's voice ceased. A deathly silence spread over Mission Control.
  Notice that the dash replaces the full stop, which is not needed.
- Dots (…): Use three dots at the end of a sentence if you wish readers to imagine the rest of the action, or to show that time is passing:
  Between us we swung the body of the murdered crook far out into the river. The evil eyes of an alligator glinted greedily…
  The posh name for these dots is an 'ellipsis'.

Punctuation within sentences

The comma (,)

Commas are used wherever a reader ought to pause. You must use a comma:

- to separate words or phrases in a list:
  My newly bought bargain car had leather seats, electric windows, central door locking, air conditioning – but no brakes. Slowly, silently, smoothly, it rolled into the river.
- to separate words or phrases in a sentence:
  The car dealer, Ted Smart, watched it all with a sly smile. He told me, with a casual shrug, that he wouldn't refund my money.
- to separate clauses in a sentence:
  He added, while my face turned a shade of purple, that I was a fool.
  I tried to reason with him, but Smart just went on grinning.
  But you don't need a comma when the subject is the same for both clauses:
  I tried to stop myself but just couldn't help punching him on the nose.
- when a person being spoken to is addressed by a name:
  Pick yourself up, Mr Smart! How do you like that, Smarty!
- with adverbs and adverb phrases that modify the

whole sentence (words like however,
nevertheless, therefore, of course, in fact, for
instance, etc.):
Of course, Smart didn't stay down for long.
• in direct speech:
'OK,' he muttered, 'you can have your money back.'
For more on direct speech, see page 66.

The semi-colon (;) The semi-colon is less popular than it used to be,
but can be very useful. You can use it:
• to link two or more simple sentences without
using a conjunction. You would only use a semi-
colon for this if the second sentence links very
strongly with the first:
*The bandit, Sal Elastico, left the court for the
cells; he knew the way. The robber had hoped
for probation; instead, Elastico was going down
for a long stretch.*
• when a number of long subordinate clauses
relate to the same verb:
*At yesterday's assembly, the headteacher said that
she was particularly pleased that the table manners
at lunchtime were much more polite; that the
school team had won their soccer match; that the
behaviour in the playground had improved.*
Each of these clauses relates to the verb 'said'.
• to punctuate long lists where individual items
already require the use of a comma:
*The four disciples closest to Jesus were: Peter,
known also by the names Simon and Cephas;
James, the first of the disciples to be martyred;
John, James's brother, sometimes referred to as
'the disciple whom Jesus loved'; and Andrew,
Simon Peter's brother.*
• in balanced sentences where the same verb
applies to both clauses and is omitted in the
second clause:
*My grandad keeps ferrets; my grandma
poisonous snakes.*

The colon (:)

The colon usually indicates that some example, explanation or list is to follow. You can use it:
- to introduce a list or example (like this one)
- to separate two statements where the second explains the first:

  Many workers were late this morning: the fog caused delays on the roads.
- to introduce a lengthy quotation
- to punctuate speech in plays (see page 68 for more on this).

The dash (–)

Experts in the English language do not always approve of the dash, but it can be very useful. Most often used in recording spoken English, it can show:
- an abrupt change of thought:

  Let's talk about bananas – no, perhaps we'll cover pineapples first.
- to set off strong, additional ideas inserted into a sentence (i.e. those more forceful than we would use commas for):

  My advice – if you will pardon my bluntness – is to think before you open your mouth!
  Jack was angry – nay, furious – at being interrupted in such a rude way.
- to show lengthy hesitation:

  Well – er – all I can say is – er – thanks very much!

The ellipsis (…)

Apart from ending a sentence (as mentioned on page 59), you can use three dots in a sentence to show that a word or words have been deliberately missed out.
Ellipses are often used when quotations are reprinted:

We will fight them on the beaches…we shall fight in the hills; we shall never surrender.

Brackets ()

You can use brackets to enclose any word or group of words which you put into a sentence as an afterthought, or to explain something in the sentence:

The referee (my Dad) made some unfortunate decisions. He sent me off (even though he knew Mum would be furious with him when we got home).

Remember There are three other ways of bracketing off words or groups of words in a sentence or paragraph:

- Commas:
  Mr Jones, the professional fire-eater, lives next door.
- Square brackets. These are used when quoting from a passage, to add an explanation not in the original text: *'England expects,' he [Nelson] signalled, 'every man to do his duty.'*
- Dashes:
  The film star threw a wobbly – or rather a tantrum – because her champagne was warm.

Punctuation within words

Apostrophes stand in for missing letters.

Hyphens

Hyphens are used:
- to join two or more words into a new, compound word:
  sun-tanned, up-to-date, a ten-year-old

- to separate a prefix from its root word in order to avoid ugly letter combinations:
  co-ordinate, pre-eminent, de-ice, will-less
- in order to avoid confusion with an existing word:
  re-cover = fit new cover / *recover* = return to normal
- when coupled with capital letters:
  U-turn, T-junction, un-American, pre-Victorian.

Remember The rules about the use of hyphens tend to change as time goes by. Always check with a good and up-to-date dictionary.

Apostrophes

Apostrophes are used:
- to indicate omitted letters:
  can't, won't, let's, I'll, that's
- to show possession:
  the girl's pens (the pens of the girl); *the girls' pens* (the pens of the girls)
  the princess's jewels (the jewels of the princess); *the princesses' jewels* (the jewels of the princesses)
  the woman's eyes (the eyes of the woman); *the women's eyes* (the eyes of the women)

Remember Possessive apostrophes are very simple to place correctly. Don't bother thinking if the owner is singular or plural! Just say to yourself, 'Who (or what) does the [object's name] belong to?' Then put the apostrophe straight after the owner.

Example 1: *The dog's bone. (one dog)*
  Your question: Who does the bone belong to?
  Answer: The dog. So put the apostrophe after 'dog'.

Example 2: *The dogs' bone. (two or more dogs)*
  Question: Who does the bone belong to?
  Answer: The dogs. Put the apostrophe after 'dogs'. Easy!!!

There are some other apostrophe rules:

1. Where adding *'s* to a noun produces an ugly or difficult sound, the *s* is dropped:

   Moses' sister (Moses's is ugly)
   Brutus' wife (not Brutus's)

2. We use apostrophes to show duration of time:

   in a week's time; two weeks' holiday

   The same rules apply for where to insert the apostrophe (see box on page 64).

3. We use apostrophes to form plurals of letters of the alphabet and words which do not normally have a plural form:

   p's and q's, if's and but's
   There are too many and's in that sentence.

Full stops

We often use full stops to show that a word has been abbreviated:

a.m., Feb., etc., Man. City, approx.

But when the first and last letters are included in the abbreviation, you do not need a full stop:

Dr, maths, Man. Utd, Mrs

Punctuation of speech

Quotation marks enclose a speaker's words.

'OK class ... it's home time,' said Mrs Sluggit.

Quotation marks (' ' or " "), also known as inverted commas or speech marks, are used in writing to mark the actual words used by a speaker. These words are known as direct speech. When you are writing by hand, use double quotation marks (" ").

Just to confuse you

Books published in Britain – like this one – usually use single inverted commas instead of double ones. Books published in the USA, on the other hand, use double inverted commas.

These are the rules for using quotation marks:

1. Only put speech marks round the actual words spoken:
   Speech marks: *Fiona said, 'I'm hungry.'*
   (This is direct speech.)
   No speech marks: *Fiona said that she was hungry.*
   (This is reported speech.)
2. When a quotation is interrupted in mid-sentence with the speaker's, you don't need a capital letter when you restart the speech:
   'I'm so hungry,' said Fiona, 'that I could eat the fridge door.'

3. Before closing or re-opening quotation marks there must always be a point of punctuation, usually a comma or otherwise a full stop, question mark or exclamation mark (so in this example there is a comma after 'metal' and a full stop after 'healthy'):

'Eating metal,' said David, 'is not very healthy.'

4. A new paragraph should be introduced at each change of speaker. This makes it clear who is speaking:

'I'll leave the fridge door then,' said Fiona.
'You could always try chewing the cupboard,' put in David.
'No thanks!'
'Suit yourself,' said David. 'I quite like a juicy shelf now and then.'

(By the way, notice that there is a comma after 'yourself' even though David's spoken sentence has finished. The full stop only comes at the end of our sentence, after the word 'David'.)

More advanced rules

5. If one speaker continues to speak for several paragraphs, re-open quotation marks for each new paragraph, but do not close them until the end of the quotation.

6. If a speaker quotes someone else, use single quotation marks (when you are writing by hand) for the words the speaker is quoting:

"I distinctly heard the starter say 'Go'," said the athlete who had left his blocks too soon.

Books that usually use single quotation marks will use double ones for quotes within speech.

Punctuation of plays

Plays use special rules for punctuation.

DOCTOR [cheerfully]: My word!   GRIMBLE [anxiously]: Is that me?

To avoid using too many speech marks, plays have their own system of punctuation. Here is a short sample script:

A doctor's waiting room. DOCTOR, a young cheerful man, enters R. GRIMBLE, a middle-aged patient, is seated L in front of doctor's desk.
DOCTOR (sitting down): Now, how are your broken ribs coming along, Mr Grimble?
GRIMBLE (anxiously): Well, I keep getting this stitch in my side!
DOCTOR (cheerfully): Good, that shows the bones are knitting!

These are the rules:
1. Descriptions of the setting and position of actors are printed in italics. (Use square brackets [ ] if you are writing by hand.)
2. Put characters' names in capital letters.
3. All movement and voice directions go in brackets.
4. Don't use quotation marks unless a character is quoting direct speech.

Punctuation in maths

Commas or spaces are often used to make large numbers easier to read:

12,345,063 or 12 345 063

They go between every group of three digits, counting right to left from the units end.

The decimal point always goes between the units and the tenths column. When printed, it is like a full stop:

104.25

When written, it goes half way up from the base of the figures:

104·25

Section 3 **Advanced Writing Skills**

A *The paragraph*

A paragraph is a group of sentences about a single topic. In a serious essay, every sentence in a paragraph must relate to that main idea.

Every paragraph must have a main idea.

The topic sentence

In writing essay paragraphs, you should include in each one a 'topic sentence' which states clearly what that central thought is. Usually this is the opening sentence of the paragraph, but it does not have to be. Paragraphs in stories or narrative writing do not always have to have topic sentences.

Types of paragraph

There are four types of paragraph in essay writing:
- loose
- mixed
- periodic
- cyclic.

Loose paragraphs

A loose paragraph is where the topic sentence is placed at the beginning. After stating the main idea, the writer then completes the paragraph with examples or explanations. The paragraph you are reading now is an example of this.

Mixed paragraphs

A mixed paragraph is where the topic sentence is in the middle of the paragraph. Sometimes it is necessary to build up to the statement of a paragraph's main thought and then to support this statement by examples or to expand upon it.

Periodic paragraphs

A periodic paragraph has its topic sentence at the end. This enables the main thought of the paragraph to be logically developed, so that when the topic sentence is reached it can be readily understood and therefore better remembered.

Remember A periodic paragraph, immediately followed by a loose paragraph, can be a useful device for connecting paragraphs.

Cyclic paragraphs

A cyclic paragraph begins and ends with the topic sentence (or two versions of it). Stating the main thought again helps to reinforce the point you are making and also acts as a useful reminder, especially if the paragraph is a long one.

Writing a paragraph

Starting off

If you are writing an essay, start work on each paragraph by writing your topic sentence. Keep it constantly in mind as the paragraph develops. This doesn't mean you have to leave the topic sentence at the beginning. You can decide where to place it once the paragraph has taken shape.

Patterns within paragraphs

Each paragraph should have a pattern or sequence of thought which keeps it together as an unit. Here are some examples:

Describing paragraphs

You can begin with a general description and gradually focus onto one person or thing:

The primroses were over. Towards the edge of the wood where the ground became open and sloped down to an old fence and a brambley ditch beyond, only a few fading patches of pale yellow still showed among the dog's mercury and oak-tree roots. On the other side of the fence, the upper part of the field was full of rabbit holes...
— *Opening lines of* Watership Down *by Richard Adams*

Alternatively you can begin with something particular, then set it within its general surroundings:

The great fish moved silently through the night water, propelled by short sweeps of its crescent tail. The mouth was open just enough to permit a rush of water over the gills. The land seemed almost as dark as the water, for there was no moon...
— *Opening lines of* Jaws *by Peter Benchley*

Tip

You could also help unify a describing paragraph by concentrating on colours, sounds, smells etc.

Time sequence paragraphs

The simplest kind of pattern is where a series of events follow in sequence. Try to avoid obvious paragraphs like this:

I woke up ... got out of bed ... dressed and had breakfast.

This is much more interesting:

The wash-basins were in the boys' cloakroom just outside the main hall. I got most of the paint off and as I was drying my hands that's when it happened. I don't know what came over me. As soon as I saw that balaclava lying there on the floor, I decided to pinch it. I couldn't help it. I just knew that this was my only chance. I've never pinched anything before – I don't think I have, but I didn't think of this as ... well ... I don't even like saying it – but ... well stealing. I just did it.

   – *From* The Balaclava Story *by George Layton*

Explaining paragraphs

Some paragraphs explain how something works or what something means. If you want your reader to understand an explanation, you must do two things:

- Keep it simple! Concentrate on the bare essentials. Cut out any waffle.
- Make sure that each idea or fact leads logically to the next one.

Paragraphs with a theme

A paragraph in an essay or other formal piece of writing should have a central idea and ought to contain a topic sentence saying what this theme is. Your choice of words, the way you construct each sentence and the way you use figures of speech (see page 84) should all help to make the theme clear.

Using connectives

Connectives hold a sentence or paragraph together.

Connectives also hold other things together.

Connectives are words and phrases that help connect one sentence with another as the reader reads them. Used between sentences, they help to give the paragraph a united style. Used between paragraphs, they help the whole piece of writing to flow. Here are some ideas for using connectives:

Between sentences

- Adverbs such as 'although', 'however', 'therefore', 'nevertheless', etc., relate one sentence to the next:

  Some people say the moon is made of green cheese. However, no mice have yet launched an expedition there.

  Some people say the moon is made of green cheese. Nevertheless, I think that mature Cheddar is more likely.

  Although some people say the moon is made of green cheese, Neil Armstrong and his pals couldn't even find a bit of rind.

- You can also use phrases (e.g. 'for instance', 'for example', 'another case is', 'on the other hand') to link sentences.

- Adverbs of time ('then', 'after this', 'meanwhile', 'now', 'consequently', etc.) are useful connectives. However, do not over-use them!

- The conjunctions 'and', 'but', 'because' may open a sentence to help pull the paragraph together.
- Although it is usually bad style to repeat yourself in writing, deliberate repetition of a word can unify a passage and give emphasis:

The other four stared at me in wonder. Then, as the sheer genius of the plot began to sink in, they all started grinning. They slapped me on the back. They cheered me and danced around the classroom. 'We'll do it today!' they cried. 'We'll do it on the way home! YOU had the idea, 'they said to me, 'so YOU can be the one to put the mouse in the jar!'

– From Boy *by Roald Dahl*

Between paragraphs
- Where a topic sentence (see page 70) ends one paragraph, you can write a topic sentence in a similar style to begin the next paragraph.
- Where appropriate, use the adverbial phrase 'In the same way…' to begin a new paragraph.

Sentence variation

Check your sentences for length.

When you have finished your first version of a paragraph, check it for:
- Sentence length: Are your sentences varied in length? Within each paragraph, some should be

long, some short. Some should be simple, some complex.

- Sentence type: If you use only loose sentences (see page 57) your paragraph will be dull. Bring in an occasional periodic or mixed sentence to add variety.

The writing process

'What is written without effort is in general read without pleasure.' – Dr Samuel Johnson (1709–84)

To write well, you must be prepared to draft and re-draft your work. With a word processor this is easy; if you write on computer, read through each paragraph and alter it as you go. You should also print out a draft hard copy of your work from time to time, read it thoroughly and mark the changes you need to make when you go back to the keyboard. The words you are now reading were written exactly in this way.

Even the most successful and experienced writers work away at each sentence and paragraph to get it exactly as they want it. That's why they're successful!

B *Special uses of language*
Register

Perhaps he should try a different register.

'Right! Now, first I need to know your correct point of departure. Then, please enumerate each of the stopping points en route to your destination . . .'

Register is the level at which we make our language work. A mother speaking to a four-year-old child uses language at a fairly low register. A teacher talking to Year 6 pupils uses a higher register. Two university professors discussing the Arsenal v. Liverpool game might be using a register somewhere in between. Register depends chiefly on three things:
- vocabulary
- sentence structure
- the suitability of language to a situation.

Vocabulary

In English there are many words which have similar meanings:

start: begin, commence, found, originate
tiny: small, little, minuscule, microscopic

Some of these are obviously not suitable when speaking to a child or to someone just beginning to learn English. So 'There's only a tiny drop at the bottom of the glass' is lower in register than 'A microscopic quantity of liquid remains in the flask.'

> **Remember** The lower register is not 'wrong' in any way. You need to talk to a young child more simply than you might talk to a professor.

The actual words you use should be suitable for:
- the person you are speaking to
- the topic you are discussing
- the situation you are in.

Sentence structure

Just as the words we use need to vary according to the situation, so the way we put words together in sentences may be suitable for some people, topics and situations, but not for others.

Simple sentences will keep the register low, so be ready to change your sentence patterns depending on your 'audience'. Here are some examples:

1. *I have a cat. It has two eyes. They are green. They change in different lights. Cats are quite marvellous creatures!*

2. *My cat's two green eyes change when the light changes. This is one of the reasons why cats are such marvellous creatures.*

The sentence patterns in (2) are much more complex than those in (1). The register of (2) is higher than that in (1). A higher register still might be:

3. *The green eyes of cats adapt marvellously to varying intensities of light.*

The suitability of language to a situation

Good communication rests, like a camera tripod, on three 'feet' – Content, Audience and Motivation – CAM for short. To communicate well in speech or writing, you always need to remember CAM. You must know:
- *what* you are saying (Content)
- *who* you are saying it to (Audience)
- *why* you are saying it (Motivation).

What? – The content

What you are trying to say will determine how you ought to say it. For example: figures or statistics are best not spoken; birthday wishes are best not typed (they are personal and should be hand written); an annual report is meant not to be read aloud but studied in printed form.

> **Remember** Check what is best for what you have to say – will you be speaking or writing? Would a diagram, chart or photograph help?

Who? – The audience

We can get our meaning across in many different ways. It depends on who we are dealing with. A chat with a friend is very different from an interview with the headteacher! Speaking to the class in a lesson is not the same as standing up to speak in school assembly.
Also, your audience may consist of males and females, adults and children – even, perhaps, people who know little English.

> **Remember** Before you speak or write, think who you are talking to.

Why? – The purpose

Your reason for saying something will influence how you communicate. To persuade someone, you need to speak or write in a different register and tone from when you are trying to warn them, teach them or make them laugh.

> **Remember** Make sure you match your tone to your purpose.

If one leg of the CAM tripod collapses, the whole lot collapses – so think carefully about the What? Why? and Whom?, and get all three right!

Standard English

Standard English is a dialect we can all understand.

'Luv a duck. Then the ol' girl . . .
she fell darn the apples 'n' pears.'

Standard English is the name given to 'official' English – a type of English that follows the rules found in dictionaries and grammar books. It is the English used in business letters and serious writing. It is also the way most newsreaders speak on television.

Standard English is not the only 'correct' kind of English. Other common types, such as regional dialects, are just as suitable and worthwhile. After all, people were speaking English very successfully long before grammar books were written.

Besides, language is constantly changing, and the rules of English are not set in stone. Yesterday's 'mistakes' may well turn up in tomorrow's grammar books!

But Standard English is very useful as a sort of 'common currency', which we can all understand even if we don't usually speak it. That's why we all learn it in school.

Informal language

Idioms

Idioms are phrases that are special to a particular language and that foreign people often find hard to understand or translate. The word 'idiom' comes from the same Greek root as 'idiot' – something private and peculiar, belonging to oneself.

For example, a French person might be puzzled if you said, 'Use your loaf and get cracking!' Where's the bread? What do I crack with it?

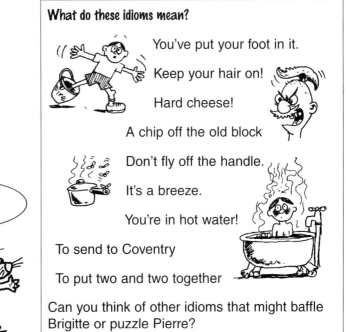

What do these idioms mean?

You've put your foot in it.

Keep your hair on!

Hard cheese!

A chip off the old block

Don't fly off the handle.

It's a breeze.

You're in hot water!

To send to Coventry

To put two and two together

Can you think of other idioms that might baffle Brigitte or puzzle Pierre?

People say the oddest things!

Remember Language is a living, changing thing, and idioms are always being invented. These days, computers get bugs and crash, and it's easy-peasy to clock Level One of Sonic.

Clichés

A cliché is an expression that has been over-used and has lost its impact and freshness. Despite this, you will often hear clichés being used on TV and radio. Listen out for them, but keep them out of your writing! Here are some examples:

first and foremost; at the end of the day; over the moon; sick as a parrot; I hear what you're saying; peace and quiet; last but not least; raining cats and dogs; hard as nails; the blushing bride; to make or break

'Cliché' is the French word for a mould – something that always produces the same shape.

Slang

Slang is the words and phrases that people use in everyday talk but which have not yet become accepted in polite or formal conversation. You certainly wouldn't use them in formal writing (except when recording dialogue or for special effects such as humour). There are four kinds of slang:

• Old word – new meaning:
  dough, bread, readies = money
  anorak = a total enthusiast with no other interests

• Foreign words not formally accepted:
  vamoose (from Mexican 'vamos') = let us go
  pronto (Spanish for prompt) = immediately, very soon

• Newly coined words:
  ginormous = gigantic + enormous
  nimbyism = a resistance to new building, etc. (from Not In My Back Yard)

• Words or phrases in place of others:
  butcher's = look (Cockney rhyming slang: butcher's hook)
  the big smoke = city

> **Rhyming slang: what do these mean?**
> Climb the apples and pears.
> Let's scarper. (from 'Scapa Flow')
> My plates are aching! (from 'plates of meat')
> Do you fancy a ball of chalk?
> Would you Adam and Eve it?
> Give us a butcher's. (from 'butcher's hook')
> Across the frog and toad.

The fact that we cannot use slang in serious conversation or writing does not mean we should reject it. Slang keeps giving new life to the language. Besides, slang words can become respectable. For instance, 'donkey' (from *dun* = 'light brown' + -*ke* = affectionate suffix) was a slang word up to a century ago.

Colloquialisms

Colloquial phrases are slang expressions which are so familiar that they are acceptable in all but the most formal of conversations. A colloquialism may also be an idiom.

He gave the driver a dirty look.
How ghastly!
She was bumped off
Are you with it?

However, colloquialisms are not usually acceptable in serious written work. If you are writing an essay, find a formal alternative.

Jargon

Jargon means the special words and phrases used in a trade, profession or any exclusive group. Jargon is not likely to be understood easily by other people outside that group:

In printer's jargon, to 'put to bed' means to place the fully checked, final version of a newspaper on the printing press, ready to 'run'.

In surfer's jargon, to 'wipe out' means to fall off or capsize.

In musician's jargon, the 'middle eight' means the middle instrumental section of a standard pop song (eight bars long).

In management jargon, 'cascading' means training or giving information to some people who later must pass it on to others.

Jargon, like all technical terms, is a form of 'shorthand'. It says something that would otherwise take much longer to explain.

> **Remember** Never use jargon with people who will not understand it.

Figures of speech

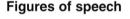

'Porky! Your room is a pigsty.'

A figure of speech is any word or phrase, perhaps an idiom, that is used in a non-literal sense – in other words, it does not mean what it literally says. For example, 'It's raining cats and dogs' doesn't mean that we have to look out for falling dalmatians each time it clouds over; 'Your bedroom is a pigsty' doesn't mean that there are grunts coming out of the wardrobe. These are the three commonest ways in which non-literal speech is used:

Figurative language
This includes words that are used every day in a non-literal way:

the hands of a clock, the foot of a mountain, saying someone is big-headed

Simile
A simile is where two things are directly compared because they share a feature in common. A word, such as 'like' or 'as', is used to draw the comparison:

as slippery as an eel; as cold as a dog's nose
My father-in-law had a face like a bag of spanners.

Beware!

There are many similes which have become clichés (see page 82):

as good as gold, as heavy as lead, as pretty as a picture . . .

It is much better style and much more fun to make up similes of your own:

as cold as a fridge in winter, as hard as my Granny's rock cakes, skin like a spotwelder's bench

---

Metaphor
Like a simile, a metaphor compares two things, but it does so more directly and without using 'like' or 'as'. The word 'metaphor' comes from a Greek word meaning to carry over, transfer:

Arnie was a man-mountain; the striker was a goal machine; the shop was a little gold mine.

We use metaphors all the time, usually without realizing it:

the key to a problem; a car ploughs into a bus queue; your brother makes a pig of himself

Remember Don't mix your metaphors. The results can be awful, or ridiculous:

We must put our best foot forward, take the bull by the horns and leave no stone unturned.

He grasped the nettle while it was hot.

Special effects

Try some special writing techniques.

There are many special techniques you can use to make your writing more interesting or effective. Whether they work or not depends on using them at the right time and in the right place, which takes practice. Here is a sample of what you can do:

Alliteration

Alliteration is the repeated use, for effect, of the same initial letter (usually a consonant) or sound. This is often used to make a phrase easy to remember.

Many book tities and advertisements use alliteration:

Charlie and the Chocolate Factory
Pride and Prejudice
Dumb and Dumber

There are also many examples in poems:

the forest's ferny floor
the stuttering rifle's rapid rattle
When fishes flew and forests walked.

Antithesis

Antithesis involves bringing together two opposite ideas into one sentence to bring out the contrast between them:

The wisest fool in Christendom (said about King James I).

No, madam, Bach is not composing; he is decomposing.

Assonance

Assonance is the rhyming of vowels (but not the consonants) within two or more words. The words involved must be close enough together to create an effect. Say these phrases to yourself, listening out for the repeated vowel sounds:

Better than voices of winds that sing

Silence and emptiness with dark stars passing

Deep Heat

Euphemism

A euphemism is an indirect or deliberately mild way of referring to something unpleasant:

death = passing away, passing on or falling asleep

murder = bumping off, rubbing out, a hit

the lavatory = bathroom, cloakroom, little girls' room

Innuendo

Innuendo is getting over your meaning by hinting or suggesting, often because you have to say something unpleasant:

That new gold watch you are wearing is remarkably like the one I lost last month!

Irony

Irony is saying something but meaning the opposite.

This is usually obvious from the speaker's tone of voice:

Teacher to dozy, inattentive class: 'You're a really bright lot this afternoon!'

Sarcasm

Sarcastic remarks are a cruel form of irony. For example, a bully might trip up another child and then say, 'Oh dear! Charlie's fallen and hurt himself!'

The word 'sarcasm' comes from the Greek meaning 'to tear at like a dog'.

Onomatopoeia

Onomatopoeia is the use of words to make the sounds they describe:

splash, squelch, buzz, pitter-patter, zoom

Proverb

A proverb is a short popular saying which teaches some lesson about life:

A stitch in time saves nine.

Beggars can't be choosers.

Section 4

Index